A BOOK *of* POETIC REFLECTIONS

Yhavina's HEART

A Book *of*
Poetic Reflections

Yhavina's HEART

Yolanda Hill McLendon

CREATION
HOUSE

Yhavina's Heart by Yhavina McLendon and Yolanda Hill McLendon
Published by Creation House
A Charisma Media Company
600 Rinehart Road
Lake Mary, Florida 32746
www.charismamedia.com

All Scripture quotations are from the King James Version of the Bible.

Design Director: Bill Johnson
Cover design by Rachel Lopez

Visit the author's website: www.YhavinasHeart.com

Library of Congress Control Number: 2011921021
International Standard Book Number: 978-1-61638-456-2

First Edition

11 12 13 14 15 — 9 8 7 6 5 4 3 2 1
Printed in the United States of America

TABLE *of* CONTENTS

Preface xi
Introduction 1
Foreword 3
Background About My Daughter 5

Poems

Let Everything That Has Breath Praise the Lord 7
The One True God 8
If They Only Knew 10
Meet God 12
When I Sit In Darkness 14
Noble Insation 16
Sinful Lullabies 18
You Big Idiot, Satan 20
The Father's Return 22
Wonderful Irony 24
You Didn't Need One 26
The Ultimate Bloody Gift 27
Blood Money 29
The Brook 31
Peace Be Still 33
Phone Call, #1 35
The Baby Talk 37
Enlightening Revolution 39
All the Glamour of War 41
Phone Call, #2 43
Fifteen Days 45
Two Pieces of Wood 47
The Tomb 53

Prayers for the Whole Person

Salvation.....57
Healing.....57
Finances..... 58
Encouragement/Anxiety/Fear..... 58
Wisdom/Direction..... 60
Spiritual Warfare/Protection..... 60
Fasting.....61
Sons and Daughters.....62

Activities for the Whole Person

Page of Single-Mindedness..... 65
Page of Growth.....67
Page of Souls..... 68
Page of Refreshing..... 69
Page of Surrender.....70
Shield of Faith.....71
Page of Encouragement..... 73
Page of Prayer.....75
Page of Edification.....76
Page of Comfort..... 77
Dreams, Visions, and Spiritual Interactions with God..... 79
About the Author.....81
Contact the Author..... 83

DEDICATION

Yhavina's Heart is lovingly dedicated to the one who inspired it, Jesus Christ, and also to Yhavina McLendon, the author. It is also dedicated to her siblings, Yelynda Rheah and Jehonathan. You loved and cared for her throughout this ordeal, thank you. To her dad, Renay, Mrs. Hill, her amazing grandmother, to her devoted godmother, Shevarn, thank you. To Shirley, I'll always remember what you did to help, thank you. To all of my loving sisters, Sheila, Sandra, and Mae, thank you. To my brothers, Spencer and Jonathan, thank you. To my dear nieces, nephews, and friends who stood with us during this time, we love and thank you.

I dedicate this book to Candice Chilson, one of Yhavina's dearest and best friends. She was relentless in assisting with Yhavina's recovery as well. Unfortunately, on November 10, 2001, a drunken driver claimed her life. There are not enough words to thank you sweet Candice. We love and miss you.

I must include you my most excellent friend, Carmen. You held up my arms and labored endlessly to help my family by whatever means necessary. While we were away, your family's presence was constant throughout this odyssey.

PREFACE

Yhavina's Heart

"THAT'S MY HEART." This is a phrase that I have often heard spoken in reference to one that is dearly loved. It is a personal statement that makes it understandable as to how someone can speak of a loved one in this way. The ability to love so strongly and assuredly is, in my opinion, the very peak of love unfeigned. This is how God loves us—without reservation or restriction.

This ring represents my commitment to my Lord and His commitment to me. It is a symbol that our relationship will always be unvarying with no regrets. The open space represents my open heart to His will for my life. The gold is the result of His hand upon my life through trials and tribulations. I have been tried and brought forth shining. He has made me a symbol of the precious element itself. The empty part is how I see myself without Him in my life. The filled part reminds me that I am complete in God. It reminds me that no matter what happens, my wholeness is in Him. My life is in Him. My heart . . . is Jesus.

INTRODUCTION

Y*havina's Heart* is a guidebook of eclectic ministry. It will take the reader on an inspirational journey through poems, prayers, scriptures, and activities. The purpose of this book is to uplift the heart, direct the soul, and feed the spirit, assisting the believer in becoming an excellent neighbor. A Bible Study-style question-and-answer section is included with each poem and includes scriptures and graceful words of encouragement. These sections invite the reader to be a part of this devotional by causing them to reflect on and note their feelings, views, and comments regarding their own kingdom work. The questions are designed to exhort the reader to reflect on God's goodness to them. These sections will also encourage the reader to be proactive in seeking a closer walk with Jesus. This anointed tool will reveal Yhavina's faith and relationship with God.

This is a unique book. There are many poetry lovers, and Yhavina's poems are a fresh approach to any devotional. The contents are gripping and hold deep messages that will minister to the inner man.

Prayers have been added to *Yhavina's Heart* as an additional ministering tool. These Scripture-based prayers are quick, sharp, and powerful because they are designed from the Father's own Word (Heb. 4:12). Whatever God says, prospers. His Word is truth, and it will never return to Him void (Isa. 5: 11). Look into Yhavina's Heart and be blessed.

FOREWORD

It had been a long day, even though it was only the early part of the afternoon. I was in misery, because I believed that I was in labor. Unfortunately, I was the only one. I had been to the hospital the week prior, the following week, and earlier the same day, for the same reason and was sent home with a sheet explaining "How to know when you are truly in labor." So there I was making the long journey back home again, miserable. Approximately ten minutes after arriving home my water broke.

Sheepish laughter emanated from a few staff members when they saw me coming in once again holding my small belly. I was in too much discomfort to care, but when one of the attending staff members told me that I did not look anywhere close to being nine-months pregnant, and that I needed to be patient with the process, I felt worse. When I announced that my water had broken, their silence became louder than their laughter. I was so thankful when I found myself being wheeled to the labor and delivery floor.

A day and a half later, on May 4, 1984, Yhavina was born. When I first saw my daughter she had a lovely and peaceful countenance. I knew that once again I had been blessed with a very special gift. She weighed barely four pounds and was very petite. I was told that we would be discharged on different dates unless they could get her weight up to five pounds before I left. I began to feel depressed since I was to be discharged within two days. My family encouraged me and we began to pray. As soon as I felt the burden lift, I remember being given a message from the nursery that Yhavina was not accepting her feedings. I immediately called the devil a liar because I realized that she was under attack. I began to rejoice in the Lord because I knew that my prayers had been answered and that God was going to use her for His glory and He did.

Yhavina was a child who attained much enjoyment from small things. Her first word was not *Mommy* or *Daddy,* but *Jesus.* She was eight months old when she began to walk. I was amazed by her agility and precision. What a fast learner. Perhaps she was trying to get an early start on God's will for her life. Maybe she knew that her visit to this world would be a short one.

Yhavina frequently told me that she was a day seizer and that she would do all that she could for God's glory while the opportunity was present. My daughter often spoke of her love and admiration for her Savior, not only in words, but also in deeds. The sincerity and commitment that she exemplified at such a young age gripped my heart. I have great peace in knowing that Yhavina's lifestyle followed through with her statement of faith.

God opened the door for every desire of Yhavina's heart to be accomplished. One of those desires was to create a poetry book that would minister to those who needed it. Be blessed by what you read, for it is truly her heart.

BACKGROUND ABOUT MY DAUGHTER

LYING BESIDE ME staring up at the ceiling with her beautiful, almond-shaped eyes, she smiled. The smile grew very wide then paused still in place. There was so much joy in her little face, but I wish that I knew what she was looking at up there. My little girl, Yhavina, did this on the Friday evening of May 4, 1984, the day that she was born. I did not find this normal for a newborn, but then she had been peculiar since before her birth and continued to be throughout her life.

Yhavina rarely cried as a baby and throughout her toddler and little-girl/big-girl years, she greeted me daily with smiles and excelled in school. My daughter wasted no time with her witness for Christ. She took her Bible to school every day and told her friends about Jesus. She would always ask if I could pick up her friends for church. After clearing it with their parents, I did. By the time she entered middle school, it was announced in church that the front pew looked like Noah's ark because there were so many youth in service. Yhavina continued to serve the Lord throughout these years and was very involved in church, outreach, and school.

There is an amazing satisfaction that a mother gets from seeing all of her children saved, serving God, and being well. However, August 8, 2000, was the last day that I would see them all together and having fun in what I called a normal way. Yhavina was diagnosed with a brain tumor that took her through an odyssey of events. Throughout the whole ordeal, she never complained, never became bitter, and never kept silent. She continually praised and witnessed to hospital staff, family, friends, and even strangers about God's goodness to her. I was especially amazed when complete strangers asked if they could come into her room and just sit down for a little while because they felt something wonderful when passing by. I even received a phone call (I do not know how she attained my number) from a woman who I had never met in my life. She told me that her dad had been a patient on the same floor as my daughter and that Yhavina had been such a blessing to him. At the time, my daughter was bedridden and could hardly talk. I thought that I knew God's love and grace pretty well until my daughter became ill. I then began to see Him in a way that she always had; that is why she never lost her peace.

Yhavina loved Jesus and lived each day to the fullest. She was an excellent student, Encouragement Chaplain at Oral Roberts University, an annual Fine Arts Festival participant (hosted by the Assemblies of God church), the vice president of her high school Thespian Club, a Shakespeare Famous Poet, a Thurgood Marshall Achiever, a three-time Who's Who Among American High School Students recipient, and National Dean's List recipient. Yhavina was a member of the King's Kids Choir, the Spirit Life Ensemble, the Bethel Temple Ensemble, and the Burnett Middle School Choir. She was also a contestant in the Miss Florida Teen Coed Pageant, a songwriter, a gospel recorder, an actress in several plays and three popular productions. She is the author of *Arouse the Dawn*, a Christian fantasy book, and a published poet. She was an active youth group member and worked as a church volunteer. She also worked on the weekends as fashion model/recruiter for a popular modeling agency. Yhavina also appears in the opening credits for the *Meet God* television show for Star Ministries.

My daughter became ill in the fall of 2000, but confirmed that she would be a witness regardless of her physical condition. She continued to minister from her hospital bed and wrote *Arouse the Dawn* while undergoing chemotherapy, which was miraculous. God blessed her to complete it. Yhavina stated that she wanted people to know that Jesus reigns in every universe. In the early spring of 2004 she went to live with Him. She was blessed with nineteen earthly years.

POEMS

I wrote this poem on July 6, 1997, as I thought about the glory of the Lord.

Let Everything That Has Breath Praise the Lord

The rain sings His praises
The birds declare His love
The trees lift their branches
To worship the Father above

The grass grows with such pace
Each strand wants to be the first
To touch His face

The wind whispers hallelujah
The sun shines in the sky
To remind us all of the sacrifice
Made by the Lord Most High

The thunder shouts His praise
The moon tells His glory
The stars chat in the heavens
Telling that old Christmas story

So accept God into your hearts
You will never ever be bored
and from the mountains of your hearts
You'll sing the praises of the Lord.

> The heavens declare the glory of God, and the firmament sheweth his handiwork
>
> —Psalm 19:1

List three wonders that will prove God's glory in the earth. Explain how.

____

____

____

Date written unknown.

The One True God

Lord I open my heart to You
I know that Your Word is true
Some have tried so many other ways to love

And be loved back, too
But I know that I can never be happy
With an idol in place of You

For You are the one true God
The only one true God
You have saved me
You have given me a new life
Yes
You are the one true God

I have made up my mind to stay
With my eyes fixed upon You
Cause nothing in this world
Could suffice for what You do
And even if the world should fall away
I will never turn my back on You
For You would never turn your back on me.

Have you made the heavenly Father Lord of your entire life? If not, record your reason below.

What are some things that you can do daily to know God in a more intimate way?

____

____

____

____

____

If you have already made the heavenly Father Lord of your entire life, go to the *Page of Single-Mindedness* at the end of this devotional. Record in sentences or in one word what you did for the day to be single-minded towards God. Look up the scriptures noted, and then fill in the blanks and meditate on them.

____

____

____

____

____

> Jesus said unto him, Thou shalt love the Lord thy God with all thy heart, and with all thy soul and with all thy mind. This is the first and great commandment.
>
> —Matthew 22:37–38

I wrote this poem after thinking about the great sacrifice of my Savior.

If They Only Knew

If they only knew who they were nailing to the cross
They would have repented so that their souls would not be lost

If they only knew who they were spitting at and mocking
The response of remorse would have been shocking

If they only knew that at that moment someone was saving their life
If they only knew that, that someone was Jesus Christ

They would have fallen down in a fit of guilt
Letting go of the shrine of hatred they had built

"Father, forgive them for they know not what they do."
Was the plea of this great Man, who spoke nothing but the truth

If Pilate only knew that he was sending his Savior to death
The shock would have completely taken away his breath

But they did it anyway
And much to their dismay

The sun turned to darkness, the moon turned to blood
The temple curtain ripped in half, and then they understood

A certain soldier looked at the Man lying dead on the cross
With his voice full of awe he said, "Surely, this was the Son of God."

I have great news my friends
Jesus rose again and He's seated at the right hand of God

He gave His life once to forgive all sin
So let's not crucify Him again.

Below write down at least two blinders that have fallen from your eyes since your conversion.

____

____

____

____

____

Write about how you see your life now, on the *Page of Growth,* located at the end of this devotional.

> Therefore if any man be in Christ, he is a new creature. Old things are passed away; behold all things are become new.
>
> —2 Corinthians 5:17

I wrote this poem in 1998. I was asked to write an introduction rap song for the Meet God *Christian television series.*

Meet God

I want to introduce you to a friend of mine
He'll never leave you lonely and He's always on time
He wants to be your friend and take care of you
Why don't you shake His hand and say, "How do you do?"

You say, "I'll meet Him later. I've got so much to do."
What do I have to say to get through to you?
You're playing with your life, scared of what friends might say
Don't make yourself regret it on that great and final day

Meet God, He'll always be right by your side
He'll guide you all the way to everlasting life.

If you are a person governed by timidity or a fear of man, remember that the Gospel is each Christian's responsibility. Please share it. As saints it is more important for us to obey the Word of God than to cater to any idiosyncrasy or fear. We must be a witness and do all we can to compel men, women, boys and girls to meet God (Mark 16:15).

List the names of some people you know who have not yet met God. Pray faithfully over them every day. As each person enters into the kingdom, draw a line through his or her name, and then record it on the *Page of Souls* at the end of this devotional.

1. ______________________________

2. ______________________________

3. ______________________________

4. ______________________________

5. ______________________________

6. ______________________________

7. ______________________________

8. ______________________________

9. ______________________________

10. ______________________________

The angels in Heaven are rejoicing!

> Likewise, I say unto you, there is joy in the presence of the angels of God over one sinner that repenteth.
>
> —Luke 15:10

> That if thou shalt confess with thy mouth the Lord Jesus, and shalt believe in thine heart that God hath raised him from the dead, thou shalt be saved. For with the heart man believeth unto righteousness, and with the mouth confession is made unto salvation.
>
> —Romans 10:9–10

I do not recall the date when I wrote this poem, but may God be glorified by it.

When I Sit In Darkness

When I sit in darkness
And I cannot see
The Lord will go before
And be a light unto me

For I am only human
But He is God above
He will come to shelter me
With everlasting love

I often sin
But He forgives
I shall die
But He only lives

If you are ever feeling sad
Call on God
He will make you glad.

What passages in the Bible come to mind when you read this message? Reflect back on a time when God's light shined through a dark period in your life. Write about it below and then read it. Encourage yourself in His faithfulness. List other times that God has given you deliverance on the *Page of Refreshing* at the end of this devotional.

___

___

___

___

___

The Lord is my light and my salvation; whom shall I fear?

—Psalm 27:1

In my distress I called upon the Lord and cried unto my God: he heard my voice out of his temple, and my cry came before him, even into His ears.... For thou wilt light my candle: the Lord my God will enlighten my darkness.

—Psalm 18:6; 28

But if we walk in the light, as he is in the light, we have fellowship one with another, and the blood of Jesus Christ his Son cleanseth us from all sin.

1 John 1:7

I wrote this poem on June 7, 2002, as a warning to all those who only live for the moment. It is for those who never consider the future or the consequences of a life selfishly lived.

Noble Insation

Here, I make my abode
Tormented in this layer of hell
Suffering day and night
Permanently there to dwell

No one comes to relieve me
Or give a comforting word
There is nothing but loss and hopelessness
In vain I pray to the Lord

A man with a hoary head arrives
He is terrified beyond natural belief
He struggles to no avail
For bound in shackles is he

I lament my previous disillusion
The greed of self-evolvement
The wirra of my life
Which brought expedient punishment

Consumed in self-love
Overcome by wanting everything
I refused to give solace
Not knowing the agony my choice would bring

Now here I am crying out for mercy
Deftly I am refused
The verdict on my sin is deemed justly
In hell I stay, my chances used.

Many of us have riches, but we must always be careful to not allow our riches to have us. We must be willing to do well, and be rich in good works first (1 Timothy 6:18). Do you know someone who regularly dreams about winning the lottery? Or maybe you know someone who frequently loses money on get-rich-quick schemes. How can you use this message to minister to others? Does this message apply to you? How can you use this message to minister to yourself?

____

____

____

____

____

> But they that will be rich fall into temptation and a snare, and into many foolish and hurtful lusts, which drown men in destruction and perdition. Charge them that are rich in this world, that they be not highminded, nor trust in uncertain riches, but in the living God, who giveth us richly all things to enjoy.
>
> —1 Timothy 6:9; 17

Read St. Luke 16:19–31, then go to the *Page of Surrender* and journal your thoughts.

I wrote this poem on March 8, 2002. Mom told me about a poetry contest being advertised in the local newspaper. This poem won. I was given the opportunity to participate in the Famous Poets Society Contest. I read my poem, "Blood Money" to the judges. I came home with a William Shakespeare medallion, and a trophy. "Blood Money" was scheduled to be printed in the 2003 edition of Today's Famous Poets poetry book, On the Wings of Pegasus.

Sinful Lullabies

The weight of the Earth
Settles o'er my eyes
Gratefully I shut them
Under purple skies

Conscious to my unconsciousness
I feel a presence approach
His eyes the purest I have seen
His robe white as snow

Silver and gold he offers
Fame He is willing to give
He only bids me serve Him
To daily for Him live

His terms of fame are murky
Yet pleasing to the flesh
His riches are not without murder
And cruelty when at best

With gusto I reject Him
His countenance isn't right
I hastily abandon
The sinful lullaby
That sang to me all night.

Probably every Christian has had the experience of someone entering his or her lives and misrepresenting who he or she really was. More than likely that person was an enemy with an ulterior motive. The prayer of discernment will help to reveal the identity of angels of light. Have you been tempted recently? Are you being tempted right now? Read the scriptures below, and then go to the *Shield of Faith Page* to receive strengthening from God's plan during times of testing.

> Satan himself is transformed into an angel of light.
>
> —2 Corinthians 11:14

> Submit yourselves therefore to God. Resist the devil, and he will flee from you.
>
> —James 4:7

> The Lord knoweth how to deliver the godly out of temptations.
>
> —2 Peter 2:9

> Blessed is the man that endureth temptation: for when he is tried, he shall receive the crown of life, which the Lord hath promised to them that love him.
>
> —James 1:12

I wrote this poem/skit on March 14, 2000, after praising God for His magnificent power.

You Big Idiot, Satan!

No Satan! No Way! I'm not playing with you today!
What do I look like an idiot? No. I'm just not having it!
Why would I follow you in the first place, and bring my soul shame and disgrace?
Stop me if I'm wrong, but remind me again. Weren't you the one kicked out of heaven?
Did you actually think that "you" were all powerful, holy, mighty, and unconquerable?
You thought God was wrong and you were right? I'm gonna be laughing at you all night!
The look on your face when He threw you out must have been hilarious to talk about!
I'll bet you felt cheap. I'll bet you felt crummy. I would too if I were a big dummy.
Well, it's time for you to go now. You really shouldn't have come.
I'm about to scare your pants off. I'm about to make you run.
Here it comes. I'm praying to the Lord. I feel a verse coming on. I'm about to quote the Word:

> Submit yourself therefore to God, resist the devil and he will flee.
> —JAMES 4:7

Hey! Quit grabbing at me!
Satan is defeated! No one even cheated.
God is exalted. He found my soul and bought it.
I have authority over Satan. I…I…(looks around, but the devil is gone)
Guess he couldn't take it.

Think about a time when the enemy came to manipulate you, but you stood your ground and claimed the victory. Share your testimony to encourage someone who may be going through a similar situation.

____

____

Go to the *Page of Encouragement* at the end of this devotional to find spirit- building scriptures to pass on to the next conqueror.

> Blessed be God, even the Father of our Lord Jesus Christ … the God of all comfort. Who comforteth us in all our tribulation, that we may be able to comfort them which are in any trouble, by the comfort wherewith we ourselves are comforted of God.
>
> —2 Corinthians 1:3–4

> Finally, my brethren, be strong in the Lord and in the power of his might. Put on the whole armor of God, that ye may be able to stand against the wiles of the devil. For we wrestle not against flesh and blood, but against principalities, against powers, against the rulers of the darkness of this world, against spiritual wickedness in high places. Wherefore take unto you the whole armor of God, that ye may be able to withstand in the evil day, and having done all, to stand. Stand therefore, having your loins girt about with truth, and having on the breastplate of righteousness; And your feet shod with the preparation of the gospel of peace. Above all, taking the shield of faith, wherewith ye shall be able to quench all the fiery darts of the wicked. And take the helmet of salvation, and the sword of the Spirit, which is the word of God: Praying always with all prayer and supplication in the Spirit, and watching thereunto with all perseverance and supplication for all saints.
>
> —Ephesians 6:10–18

> Nay, in all these things we are more than conquerors through Him that loved us.
>
> —Romans 8:37

This poem was written on June 9, 2002, after longing to be with Him.

The Father's Return

Light pierces the sky
A light brighter than the sun
Elation overtakes me
The King of kings has come

Heavenly voices ring through my ears
My heart is flooded with love
My eyes cry tears of happiness
Like a heavy rain from above

Angelic beings engulf my spirit
We then begin to rise
I take a deep breath; I'm almost there
Open my eyes, fly

I sit up in bed
Full of hope not dread
For soon I shall see
How wonderful and majestic
How truly perfected
The Father's return shall be.

What feelings of hope does this message ignite inside of you? What does it compel you to do?

____

____

____

____

____

Watch therefore, for ye know neither the day nor the hour wherein the Son of man cometh.

—Matthew 25:13

And I saw heaven opened, and behold a white horse; and he that sat upon him was called Faithful and True.

—Revelation 19:11

For the Lord himself shall descend from heaven with a shout, with the voice of the archangel, and with the trump of God: and the dead in Christ shall rise first. Then we which are alive and remain shall be caught up together with them in the clouds, to meet the Lord in the air: and so shall we ever be with the Lord.

—1 Thessalonians 4:16–17

This poem is my condensed testimony of the odyssey that occurred during my illness.

Wonderful Irony

I lay dormant on the sofa unable to move from there
The daytime gave no relief to my feelings of despair
Struggling just to open my eyes, incapable of walking
Constantly vomiting and barely, just barely talking
Diagnosed with a brain tumor when I went in for a check-up
My doctor saw I was not doing well from the neck down, but especially from the neck up
The surgery would be done the next day; my doctors said that I would not make it
I'd either die or be a vegetable, my mom was told; it was thought that I could not take it
Mama simply said that there would be an irony, I would live and not be a vegetable
Through prayer and fasting I would be okay, and for it God would be responsible
It was said that she was in denial, so one of the doctors came and told me
They got the same blunt answer, so much for diplomacy
The surgery went on as scheduled and with God I survived
My doctors were amazed, but the saints knew I'd be alive
A wonderful irony to others, a blessed miracle to Christians
I spent only four weeks in the hospital and was able to go home for Christmas
To me, this was no irony; I have faith in God
Like the scripture says, He comforts me with His staff and rod (Ps. 23:4)
This was a blessed miracle, not a wonderful irony
I am alive only because Christ lives in me.

Do you know someone who is ill? Record their names on the *Prayer Page*, and then pray over them daily.

Write about a miracle in your life or someone else's that you know. Spend time praising God for His goodness and mercy before proceeding to the next page.

____

____

____

____

____

> Praise ye the Lord. Praise the Lord, O my soul. While I live will I praise the Lord: I will sing praises unto my God while I have any being.
>
> —Psalm 146:1–2

> Praise him for his mighty acts: praise him according to his excellent greatness.
>
> —Psalm 150:2

> Now unto Him that is able to do exceeding abundantly above all that we ask or think, according to the power that worketh in us.
>
> —Ephesians 3:20

I wrote this poem on April 12, 2002, when I inquired of God and received His answer.

You Didn't Need One

Gideon beheld an angelic being when I told him to fight for Israel with only three hundred men
He needed one to encourage his faith.
Abraham looked upon angels when I told him that he would have a son in his old age
He also required help with his belief
Mary beheld an angel when she was told that she would carry the Messiah
That message required physical proof
An angel visited Daniel after twenty-one days of praying for an adulterous nation
His strengthening was a necessity after that
Why weren't you amazed by an angelic appearance on your deathbed?
You were never there
Why didn't the host of heaven light up your hospital room?
My children were already on the job
Why weren't you encouraged by heavenly beings?
You were already encouraging others
Why didn't you see an angel?
You didn't need one.

What moves you about this message?

____

____

____

____

> My grace is sufficient for thee: for my strength is made perfect in weakness. Most gladly therefore will I rather glory in my infirmities, that the power of Christ may rest upon me.
>
> —2 CORINTHIANS 12:9

I dictated this poem to my sister on March 2, 2003. I lay in bed desiring to be used to inspire others, no matter what condition that I am in, well or ill.

The Ultimate Bloody Gift

Here I lay on my bed gagging and wheezing
Seeing double and my bones literally freezing

I received a package that came from the Godhead
Good news, healing is the children's bread

Jesus shed His blood so that I would be well
I still felt horrible, but what was that smell

The aroma was delicious; it gave a peaceful feeling
The sight of bread filled me with elation, knowing was for my healing

The loaf was drenched in something red
Though being blood, it was not morbid

I enthusiastically consumed every bite, how satisfying
Bittersweet, yet heavenly, like the heart of wounded Jesus

I was completely healed so I got out of bed
Stuffed with the healing I had just been fed, in the form of bread

I was about to cover the package back up and walk away without a care
When I was taken aback ... the loaf was still there

A little of His word would have been enough, but God had given much more
My cup runneth o'er, in this case, who for?

Jesus came to heal all of God's children, at the miraculous emblem I stared

Healing is the children's bread, so I went out to share.

It is easy to worship God "in season," when everything is going well. However, due to stress and worry it can sometimes be a bit more difficult to worship when life serves an "off season." In any case, just praise. He is with you. He is indeed touched with the feelings of our infirmities (Heb. 4:15). Build yourselves up on your most holy faith (Jude 1:20). Know that you are not alone and stand.

> Preach the word; be instant in season, out of season; reprove, rebuke, exhort with all longsuffering and doctrine.
>
> —2 TIMOTHY 4:2

> For the word of God is quick, and powerful, and sharper than any twoedged sword, piercing even to the dividing asunder of soul and spirit, and of the joints and marrow, and is a discerner of the thoughts and intents of the heart.
>
> —HEBREWS 4:12

> Beloved, think it not strange concerning the fiery trial which is to try you, as though some strange thing happened unto you: But rejoice, inasmuch as ye are partakers of Christ's sufferings; that, when his glory shall be revealed, ye may be glad also with exceeding joy.
>
> —1 PETER 4:12

I read "Blood Money" at the 2002 Famous Poets Contest. After pondering the great sacrifice that Jesus Christ paid for our sins, I wrote this poem in the hotel room the day of the contest. I wanted to share with the judges and contestants what Christ had done for everyone, and this poem was the best way to do it. "Blood Money" was published in the Shakespeare's Famous Poets *book, 2003 Edition.*

Blood Money

Up the dreary hill He trudged
Over rocks and gravel drug
The price demanded for me
The merchandise of man was not free

Sin drove a hard bargain
I could not pay with doves and rams
So God consented to acquit me
With the blood of His lamb

Deep and hard the nails were driven
A sword savagely pierced His side
My payment spilt to the ground
As the ransom giver died.

What has Christ's blood sacrifice meant to you?

____

____

____

____

____

How does the title, "Blood Money" deepen your view of what happened at Calvary? Write about it in very explicit words, and then read St. Matthew, chapter 27.

____

His visage was so marred more than any man, and his form more than the sons of men.

—Isaiah 52:14

Surely he hath borne our griefs, and carried our sorrows: yet we did esteem him stricken, smitten of God, and afflicted. But he was wounded for our transgressions, he was bruised for our iniquities: the chastisement of our peace was upon him; and with his stripes we are healed. All we like sheep have gone astray; we have turned every one to his own way; and the Lord hath laid on him the iniquity of us all. He was oppressed, and he was afflicted, yet he opened not his mouth: he is brought as a lamb to the slaughter, and as a sheep before her shearers is dumb, so he openeth not his mouth. He was taken from prison and from judgment: and who shall declare his generation? for he was cut off out of the land of the living: for the transgression of my people was he stricken. And he made his grave with the wicked, and with the rich in his death; because he had done no violence, neither was any deceit in his mouth. Yet it pleased the Lord to bruise him; he hath put him to grief: when thou shalt make his soul an offering for sin, he shall see his seed, he shall prolong his days, and the pleasure of the Lord shall prosper in his hand. He shall see of the travail of his soul, and shall be satisfied: by his knowledge shall my righteous servant justify many; for he shall bear their iniquities. Therefore will I divide him a portion with the great, and he shall divide the spoil with the strong; because he hath poured out his soul unto death: and he was numbered with the transgressors; and he bare the sin of many, and made intercession for the transgressors.

—Isaiah 53:4–12

I wrote this poem one evening while thinking of how God is my all in all.

The Brook

Lonely hearts dying in the night
Distant hearts with no strength to fight
Every lowly soul with no where to look
Go to the Brook

Fallen children sick and sore
Silent blind ones looking for a door
Atheistic corpses hanging by a hook
Flock to the Brook

Dead and dying precious ones
Hungry, hurting bleeding ones
Pitiful generation who by life have been shook
Hurry I say! Hurry to the Brook

There you'll find happiness, life and joy
Love and completeness for every girl and boy
The Brook will surround you and lift you up
Above all the turmoil this world can sum up

So hopeless, helpless, pleading ones
Desperate, dying, needing ones
Seeking crying, unreceiving ones
Surrender to the Brook.

Is there anything pressing against your mind, weighing you down? If so, read the poem again. Lay your burdens on the one who was meant to carry them. Jesus is the burden bearer, not us.

___

___

___

___

___

Thou wilt keep him perfect peace, whose mind is stayed on thee: because he trusteth in thee.

—Isaiah 26:3

Fear thou not; for I am with thee: be not dismayed; for I am thy God. I will strengthen thee; yea, I will help thee; yea, I will uphold thee with the right hand of my righteousness.

—Isaiah 41:10

Come unto me, all ye that labour and are heavy laden, and I will give you rest. Take my yoke upon you, and learn of me; for I am meek and lowly in heart: and ye shall find rest unto your souls. For my yoke is easy, and my burden is light.

—Matthew 11:28–30

Let not your heart be troubled: ye believe in God, believe also in me. In my Father's house are many mansions: if it were not so, I would have told you. I go to prepare a place for you. And if I go and prepare a place for you, I will come again, and receive you unto myself; that where I am, there ye may be also.

—John 14:1–3

I wrote this poem one evening in 1999 after a heavenly inspiration.

Peace Be Still

Twas a horrid night
The waves crashed to and fro
This would surely be the death
Of the men who rowed in vain

Though the storm was chaotic
And the winds swift and shrill
A determined voice was heard over them
Which cried, "Peace be still!"

Today countries have many conflicts
The cause of utter chaos
Indignant voices shout curses aloud
And war begets a massive loss

Poverty provides a bleak future
Life holds no meaning
What is wanted is taken by force
For begging is demeaning

Yet even though the storm of poverty grows
And the antics of war kill
We must stand in the midst of chaos
And cry, "Peace be still!"

Take a deep breath and exhale slowly. Rejoice in God, your savior. Think back on how He has held onto you when it seemed that you were hanging by a thread. Think about the times that He has used the storm to your advantage. Now look at the passage below. See how Jesus made light of the storm? Notice how He invited Peter to join him, so that they could walk on the water and through the storm together. Walk towards Jesus in faith. Do not look around you. Stay focused until you reach him.

But the ship was now in the midst of the sea, tossed with waves: for the wind was contrary. And in the fourth watch of the night

> Jesus went unto them, walking on the sea. And when the disciples saw him walking on the sea, they were troubled, saying, it is a spirit,' and they cried out for fear. But straightway Jesus spake unto them, saying, "Be of good cheer, it is I; be not afraid." And Peter answered him and said, Lord, if it be thou, bid me come unto thee on the water. And he said, Come. And when Peter was come down out of the ship, he walked on the water, to go to Jesus.
>
> —MATTHEW 14:24–29

Every storm has a name, but it must bow to the One with the highest name. That is Jesus. Hallelujah!

> Wherefore, God also hath highly exalted him, and given him a name which is above every name: That at the name of Jesus every knee should bow, of things in heaven, and things in earth. and things under the earth.
>
> —PHILIPPIANS 2:9–10

To show that God is indeed greater, how would you advise a brother or sister to make light of their storm?

Go to the *Page of Edification* at the very end of this devotional and write about it.

I wrote this poem on March 5, 2002, because I believe that life can expand when one answers the phone.

Phone Call #1

I'm just about to relax
Vacation time at last
Work all adjourned
Cares to the wind cast

God is so good
I knew I'd have time to rest
My boss suddenly told me
That as for employees, I am best

With all the work I've done
I deserve this
Should even a flea disturb my peace
It will truly be amiss

I see a child crying
The phone starts ringing
The child reaches for a gun
Now the phone is deftly singing

I quickly pick up the phone
With God's help I calm the child
He says, "Thank you. My name is Eric."
And he then begins to smile.

Life expands when you answer the phone!

Some calls are wearisome (bill collector, telemarketer, etc.). Sometimes calls come at an inconvenient time. At those times it is hard to answer the phone, especially when we are busy or just tired. Do you have any suggestions that would allow for being a good neighbor, while still being true to yourself? If so, write them down and share your suggestions with others.

Let nothing be done through strife or vainglory; but in lowliness of mind let each esteem other better than themselves.

—Philippians 2:3

I wrote this poem on March 10, 2000. I thought about a few people whose kids were bossing them around, physically fighting them, and trying to control the household authority.

The Baby Talk

So here I was listening to music
Listening to the beat and just about to lose it
When I heard someone say in a voice shrill and shrieky
Hey! Get out here! I want a cookie!
Oh those words so blunt and rude
Cut me to the heart, but she hadn't understood

I was watching television, my favorite show
X-Files was on, but she was ready to go
Let's go now! Came that demanding echo
She stamped her foot and gave an impatient blow
Oh those words, so unforgiving and mean
Cut through my insides, but she didn't see it seems

I was reading a book, getting lost in my fantasies
There were singing birds and talking chimpanzees
She didn't care that it was time for sleep or that I needed a rest
She just screamed and hollered till the end and evilly gave her best
That was it. That tantrum was all
I took that girl and sat her against the wall
After a good talking to, she quieted down
There was no more screaming, bossing, having fits or running around

I taught her respect and obedience.

Spend quality time with your child today. If you do not have a child, spend time with a young relative. Visit an orphanage or maybe even a children's hospital; give away a lot of love and hugs. If you are unable to do either, spend time in prayer for this young generation. Ask God to raise up generals and captains of the faith among them that they may be mighty laborers for a great harvest of young souls.

Write down your thoughts on loving a child to life opposed to loving him/her to death.

____

____

____

____

____

> Train up a child in the way he should go: and when he is old, he will not depart from it.
>
> —Proverbs 22:6

> Lo, children are an heritage of the Lord: and the fruit of the womb is his reward.
>
> —Psalm 127:3

Sometimes adults lack respect and obedience. God asks us to humble ourselves and to come before Him as little children. By doing this, we show a willingness to submit to His will. When an adult becomes a child that God can use, we are then likened to the man who built his house upon a rock.

> The rain descended, and the floods came, and the winds blew, and beat upon that house; and it fell not: for it was founded upon a rock.
>
> —Matthew 7:24–25

I wrote this poem after thinking about technology. I wondered about the different reactions that people had to the explosion of knowledge when it hit the earth.

Enlightening Revolution

What's that you say?
The dawning of a new day
Renaissance has begun
Come out and join the fun
Oh go away
Remember the plague?
Remember how hundreds died?
I still ask myself why
What's that you speak?
Are you talking Greek?
And Roman too?
Who taught that to you?
So many people learning
For knowledge and power yearning
What's that they say?
Back to the ancient ways
The ways of the Greeks and Romans
Oh they were such smart men
Should we go back?
Move forward up the track
I don't want to paint, sew
Or watch plants grow
Nor write stories or literature
Or draw pretty, little pictures
Who would want to sail and travel
Through sand and gravel?
Or watch breathtaking sights
Each day and by night?
What? What's that you say?
People can learn to write poetry for free?
Hey! Wait for me!

What are some new things that God has brought into your life?

____

____

____

____

____

Pray for wisdom and ask God for fresh, new ideas and witty inventions that you may be an ambassador for Him in the marketplace.

> Remember ye not the former things, neither consider the things of old. Behold, I will do a new thing; now it shall spring forth; shall ye not know it? I will even make a way in the wilderness, and rivers in the desert.
>
> —Isaiah 43:18–19

> Call unto me, and I will answer thee, and shew thee great and mighty things, which thou knowest not.
>
> —Jeremiah 33:3

I wrote this poem after hearing one of my teacher's accounts of his personal experience in the Vietnam War. I gave him a copy. This is my sophomore year in high school.

All the Glamour of War

It was an okay flight, kind of long, but okay
We were all hyped to fight for the American way
They told us that we were doing a great thing
They told us of all the happiness it would bring

About all the glamour of war

Our plane landed. With high hopes we stepped off of our flight
But then I noticed that something wasn't quite right
Where was the crowd happy to see us come and rescue?
All that I saw was a land laid waste, and the air had an eerie hue

The majesty of war

We fought day and night
Bodies fell left and right
My friend, whom I loved so well
Was made immobile by a single gun shell

One second was all it took
I didn't think or stop to look
I plunged into the fighting game
Shouting curses, wildly taking aim

Oh the heartache of war

I survived those dark nights
I went back home and after my flight
I was greeted by jeers and hostility
By the country that meant so much to me

I remember the pain
I remember the gore
And now I realize
That is "all" the glamour of war.

Do you know someone who has been hardened by war? Pray a prayer of comfort over them every day. Pray for deliverance from horrific images, painful strongholds, and brokenness. Be very submissive and sensitive to the Spirit of God when ministering words to him/her. Sometimes we may misjudge a person's needs because they may be wearing a well-fitted mask, but God knows where the dry places are in their hearts and minds. He knows how to lead you there with words that will lubricate them and permeate His love, grace, and peace from the inside out.

Record on the *Page of Comfort* some things that you can do to encourage someone today.

I just wanted everyone to know that no matter how bad it gets, Jesus is always there to pull you out of your despair, so I wrote this skit.

Phone Call #2

So here it begins. I ask for forgiveness and find none. Everyone around me deserts me. I feel alone and depressed. How can I escape this tormented life? Suicide doesn't seem too bad right now. I'm sorry. I can't stop the tears from coming. My life is damaged and in turmoil, caused by the pain of knowing that those who I love do not love me. What shall become of me? Shall I be cast off into the night, into utter darkness, a mass of pain and rejection? I can't take this anymore! Surely there is someone that can resolve me.

Who is this Jesus? I've never heard of Him.

He can cleanse people of their sins you say? Well, I would like to meet this man. Take me to Him. After everything that I've suffered, this shouldn't be too hard. I've tried everything else from drugs to prostitutes, you name it, but it all left me feeling empty. OK, I'm ready and waiting to meet Him.

What do you mean I can meet Him over the phone? Jesus isn't a man? He's the Son of God? If He is the one who people say actually died and rose again, I don't think that He'd want me.

What? He accepts everybody? Uhmm…No. I don't know the exact reason for His death.

It was to wipe away our sins? That's great! Oh, how I need His forgiveness. I've done so many bad things in my life and this just seems unreal, but it is real. At last someone who will accept me. How do I meet Him?

Through a prayer? OK, let's pray. I'll repeat after you because as much as it embarrasses me, I don't know how to pray.

Dear Jesus, I know that I've done wrong. I acknowledge my sin. I'm asking You to forgive me and come into my heart. Be my

Savior and take away this pain I feel. Lord, thank You for Your sacrifice. Amen.

I feel wonderful. This is great! The load that I felt just lifted from me. There is nothing in this world that can get me down at this moment. Hello? Hello? Wait! Who are You? What's Your name? I didn't even get to thank You...Oh well, thank You, God.

"Click."

Who has God laid on your heart for you to minister to?

____

____

____

____

____

Let this mind be in you, which was also in Christ Jesus.

—PHILIPPIANS 2:5

Let him know, that he which converteth the sinner from the error of his way shall save a soul from death, and shall hide a multitude of sins.

—JAMES 5:20

I wrote this skit after thinking about the tribulation period.

Fifteen Days

Day One: I stood there wondering: Dear God, is this what I get for being Your faithful servant? Is this the thanks I get? Then I began to feel like a fool; I complain because I am going to be executed in fifteen days. He lived His whole life knowing that He would be crucified, something far worse than being beheaded.

Day Two: In a sense I'm scared, but I don't know why. I know exactly where I'm going. I hear people walking past my cell, some scream while others walk past without a care. The followers of the beast just laugh as if they were in medieval times watching the king's jester. The sight of the 666 made my bowels move.

Day Three: Only twelve days left. I can't really say that I'm anxious. I can't wait to get to heaven, but I'm not that wild about losing my head. God is with me.

Day Fourteen: The days are winding fast. The butterflies in my stomach are biting at me. I can taste my sweat. It's unusually salty. I wave my hands to keep the flies away that come through a crack in the wall. Through that crack, I can see the believers of Christ being taken to the plank. Tomorrow it will be my turn.

Day Fifteen: Dawn came sooner than I thought it would. They took me to the plank around 9:00 a.m. A desperate fool asked me if I wished to renounce my faith. I said, "No!" He looked at me with hate unimaginable. They laid me on the platform and as he was about to pull the lever to release the blade, the sky darkened and a light shone on my face. A handsome, shining man came towards me. Suddenly I was floating in the air with millions of others all across the globe.

Write down ways that you, the believer can strengthen your faith while in the midst of persecution.

And when he had opened the fifth seal, I saw under the altar the souls of them that were slain for the word of God, and for the testimony which they held: And they cried with a loud voice, saying, How long, O Lord, holy and true, dost thou not judge and avenge our blood on them that dwell on the earth? And white robes were given unto every one of them; and it was said unto them, that they should rest yet for a little season, until their fellow servants also and their brethren, that should be killed as they were, should be fulfilled.

—REVELATION 6:9–11

For the Lord himself shall descend from heaven with shout, with the voice of the archangel, and with the trump of God: and the dead in Christ shall rise first: Then we which are alive and remain shall be caught up together with them in the clouds, to meet the Lord in the air: and so shall we ever be with the Lord.

—1 THESSALONIANS 4:16–17

I wrote this skit after telling my mom that I would not have wanted to be the wood that was used to crucify Jesus.

TWO PIECES OF WOOD

Part 1:

Wood 1: "Hey, you! Yeah. You!"
Wood 2: "What?"
Wood 1: "Don't you think that the way we were chosen was kind of weird?"
Wood 2: "Yeah. I mean they spent hours looking us over. It was as if we just had to be perfect."
Wood 1: "Then they loaded us into the wagon, smiling as if they had accomplished some great feat."
Wood 2: "What did that guy mean when he said, 'he won't be ascending from this'?"
Wood 1: "I wonder what they're going to use us for."
Wood 2: "I bet we'll be a part of a house."
Wood 1: "Maybe the base. I'll bet they needed a good base."
Wood 2: "Or maybe even a chariot."
Wood 1: "Chariots aren't made of wood."
Wood 2: "Well, I'm trying to guess."
Wood 1: "Well, I guess we'll find out when we get there."
Wood 2: "Hey, the cart stopped."
Wood 1: "Great! We'll see what they're going to do when he takes us out."
The driver comes around and removes the wood from the large cart. The two pieces of wood look intently around and see that they are at the door of a small shed.
Wood 2: "What goes on in there?"
Wood 1: "I don't know, but those nails over there are crying; so I don't think that it's anything good."
The driver sets the wood down and walks towards the nails. He picks them up, and then comes back. The man lifts up one piece of wood and places it on top of the other. He walks into the shed, comes out with a hammer and then proceeds toward the nails.
Wood 2: "Uhmm, what is he doing?"
Wood 1: "Don't know; just get off."
Wood 2: "Oh yeah, as if he won't notice a piece of wood moving by…"
Both pieces of wood cry out in unison.

BANG! "OW!"
BANG!
Wood 1: "Ugh!"
Wood 2: "Oh my!"
BANG! BANG! BANG!
The man completes the task and then returns the hammer and nails to the shed.
Wood 1: "OK. Why did that hurt?"
Wood 2: "I've always been told that you couldn't feel it. That actually hurt."
Wood 1: "Look at us! Look at the way that he put us together!"
Wood 2: "We've been turned into a crucifix! They're gonna use us to crucify someone!"
Wood 1: "No wonder the nails were crying."
Wood 2: "Of all the things to be used for."
The man comes out of the shed with more nails. He puts them, along with the cross, into the cart. He then mounts and drives off.
Wood 1: "This is just great. I didn't want to be used to kill people. This is just my luck. First, I almost got left in the forest, now this. Although, somehow I think this is worse.
Wood 2: "I know. At least in the forest you would have been among friends. How about that hammer? Parts of me have been dropped and banged before, but I have never felt anything like that!"
Wood 1: "Me either. You nails are brutal."
Nails: "Sorry."
They rode on the rest of the way in silence. Thirty minutes later the cart came to a halt.
Wood 2: "We've arrived."
Wood 1: "Great."
The man lifted them out of the cart. They saw that they were at the back of a prison. A guard standing watch went into the prison, and came out with a prisoner.
Wood 2: "Whoa! Look at him."
Wood 1: "He must have done something awful to be beaten so badly."
Wood 1 takes a closer look and notices a holy glow around the figure that stood before him. He began to moan.

Wood 1: "Oh … Oh."
Wood 2: "What is it? What's wrong?"
Wood 1: "He didn't do anything."
Wood 2: "How do you know that? We just got here. Calm down."
Wood 1: "No. You don't understand. He is the Son of God."
Wood 2 looked at the prisoner for a little while, and then began to cry. He, too, saw the holy glow and recognized his Creator.
Wood 2: "Why does He look like that? Why did they do this? Are they crazy? What's wrong with them? Can't they see that He is the Creator?
The man dragged the cross over to the prisoner and told Him to carry it.
Wood 1: "Oh No!"
Jesus embraced the cross. Despite the fact that He was feeling very weak, He headed down the road. Several soldiers followed. The cross was quite large. It caused the Lord to fall a lot under the weight of it. A soldier would frequently strike Him with a whip, and then yell for Him to get up. A crowd gathered and followed the scene. They yelled also. Some yelled for Him to be released and others for Him to be crucified.
Wood 2: "These people are definitely confused."
Jesus fell again. The cross hit the ground with a thud. He seemed very weak when He got up this time. The soldiers gathered and talked amongst themselves.
Wood 1: "Ow! You'd think they would at least carry us for Him, considering the fact that He's losing so much blood. The pain we felt before won't compare to the hurt and despair we'll have when they nail Him."
As Jesus endeavored to keep going, two soldiers forced a man from the crowd to carry His cross.
Wood 2: "I know that we're getting to our destination faster now, but this is still horrible. I just hope that this will soon end for Him. Why are they doing this?"
Wood 1: "Why did they have to use us to do it?"
They came to a hill called Golgotha, known as the place of the skull. There, Jesus was laid on the cross. Two others were already there

hanging from their crosses. They stared down at the crowd, one with pleading eyes, but the other one stared through eyes of hate.

Wood 2: "Oh boy. Here it comes."

Wood 1: "Do you think that He'll fly away? He can, you know?"

Wood 2: "He doesn't look as if He's going to fly. He's just being still."

Wood 1: "Why?"

Wood 2: "I don't..."

BANG! BANG! BANG!

Wood 2 and Jesus yelled out in pain, but each for different reasons.

Wood 2: "AAH!"

Jesus: "AAH! AAH! OHHH, Father!"

Wood 2: "Alright! I'm just about to lose it here!"

The soldier went to the other side and nailed the Prisoner's other hand to the cross. He then proceeded to nail His feet to the bottom. Wood 1 and the Lord groan in anticipation.

BANG! BANG! BANG!

Wood 1: "AAH!"

Jesus: "AAH! AAHHH!"

One of the soldiers let out a sinister laugh, and then picked up a sign that read "INRI," which means, "King of the Jews." He walked toward the top of the cross.

Wood 1: "What? Are they going to nail His head too? He isn't going anywhere! They don't have to do that! NO!"

Jesus: "Ahem."

The sign was nailed to the top of the cross. The cross was then sat up and positioned into the ground. A painful cry tore from Jesus' lips as His limbs were ripped out of their sockets by the force of gravity.

Wood 2: "I feel awful. God, why is this happening?"

God, knowing that this made the wood very sad, gave them the understanding that Jesus had to take away the sins of the world.

Wood 2: "And these humans are crucifying Him?"

Wood 1: "Why is it that plants and animals act smarter than people sometimes? They're supposed to be the superior beings."

Jesus: "Father, forgive them, for they know not what they do."

The prisoner to the right of the Lord asked Him to forgive his sins. Jesus told him that he would be with Him in paradise that very day.

Wood 2: "Jesus? Jesus, why don't you just take the pain away? That way you won't feel it."
Silence.
Wood 1: "He can't hear you. He's taken on their sin and lost fellowship with God for now. Even if He had heard you, it wouldn't matter."
Jesus: "My God! My God! Why have You forsaken me?"
Wood 2: "Okay. If I were human I would faint right now."
Wood 1: "If I were human, I'd kill them all and stop this!"
After a few hours, Jesus let out a fateful cry, and then He died. Immediately there was an earthquake throughout the land. The temple curtain was ripped in two and the sun was turned to darkness. A soldier at the scene of the crucifixion looked up at the cross.
Soldier: "Surely, this was the Son of God!"
Wood 2: "Well, isn't this a fine time to come to your senses!"
Wood 1: "Oh sweet, sweet Jesus."

THE TOMB

Part II:

I TELL YOU WHAT; I knew that something was wrong from the beginning. Obviously someone had died, but that is what I was for, so it didn't bother me. There was something eerie about the atmosphere though. The air was stale. It was as if everything had frozen over. The grass and plants seemed to be drooping a little. That earthquake didn't do much in the way of helping either. I thought that everything would drop dead, especially after the sun turned dark. That just freaked me out. Other than that, I was fine, oblivious to what awaited me. Was I ever in for a shock! The weeping people came to me bearing the body of a man who had just died. I felt so sorry for them, seeing how the mother wept over her dead Son. I thought that she might choke to death on her tears. I knew that there would be crying, but this was different. What kind of man could warrant this kind of mourning? Then…I saw Him.

The wind came and blew off part of the sheet that covered His face. It was God's Son. There's no wonder as to why they were weeping so. The Lord was dead. Even though they messed Him up good, I still recognized Him, but something was strange. He had lost something. He had been beaten very badly and His hands and feet had huge scars on them. There was no reason for Him to die, so why was He about to be buried? What had gone on? Why was He crucified? Maybe there was a holy war and He got—no, I seriously doubt it. Not when God is on the job, and He is always on the job. Then I was hit with a revelation of understanding. Men couldn't cleanse themselves of their impurities, so Jesus had to do it for them. Since the wages of sin is death, there He lies.

Here is a little history, by the way. His name is Jesus, and God sent Him here, obviously. While on earth, He was a great man. Healing the sick and forgiving sins was His specialty.

They wrapped up the Lord's body and placed Him inside of me. I was honored that I was being used, but sad that He was dead. It just wasn't right. However, there was no other way. Men couldn't do it for themselves, so Jesus did it for them. This was the result of their sin. Some of them must be weeping out of guilt, I thought. After He was laid to rest, a man rolled a large stone in front of my entrance. They wept there a little longer, and then left. I felt a great sense of loss. I remembered being formed by Him. I was smaller then, but we both knew that I would grow.

Two days passed without incident. Then on the third day a couple of guards came and stood outside my entrance. That was odd. Why were they guarding a dead man? A half hour later, the ground began to shake, and then an angel of the Lord appeared. I recognized him too. It was one of the faithful angels who stood daily in the presence of God. The guards also saw Him. They started shaking and became like dead men. When I saw that, I said to myself, "Whoa!" I was mesmerized at how perfect the angel looked. Joy beamed from his eyes. His robe was a brilliant white, and his eyes were intense like lightening. The angel was magnificent and seemed to be about seven feet tall. He stood there watching the stone as it passed him, then turned his attention towards me. The stone that was placed at my entrance began to roll away. What looked like white smoke oozed out of my mouth. I was startled by the light and by the earthquake that hit just afterwards. The shock was short lived, however.

Just then He came out! I mean "He" came out! Jesus! The Son of God! The Savior of the world was alive! I was overjoyed. Jesus stood at my entrance with love beaming from His eyes. The angel and Jesus smiled at each other. The angel of the Lord bowed and praised Jesus in a language that I could not understand, and then he vanished. Jesus walked off smiling at His creation. After a while, a couple of women came to me. They did not know that Jesus had risen. I guess they were upset because they were crying, and one of them buried her head in her hands. Jesus walked up. They did not know that it was Him. The women asked Him to tell them where Jesus' body was laid. He answered so kindly. He told them that He had risen, but had not yet ascended to His Father. The women were elated. Their whole mood changed. One of them was practically doing somersaults. He told her to go and tell the others; she did. They came running into me, looking for His body. Of course, it was not here. I heard that some of them believed that He had risen; others did not.

Once again, Jesus appeared. When the disciples saw Him they praised, worshiped, laughed, and cried. This went on for a while, then Jesus said something to them and they left with excitement. I did not see anything after that, but what I heard was that Jesus was at it again: teaching and doing miracles. I also heard that when He ascended into heaven, two angels told His followers that He would be coming back soon. Well, that is it. That is all I know. This is the end of my saga, but not the end of the story.

Thank you, sweet Jesus for paying our debt in full. Hallelujah! (Rom. 8:12.)

List more blessings, spiritual and natural for which you are thankful.

____

____

____

____

____

PRAYERS *for the* WHOLE PERSON

My Prayer for Salvation:

Dear God, thank You for having mercy on me. Thank You for sending Jesus to die for my sins. Please forgive me for all of my sins, ignorance and stupidity (slow to learn my lessons). I don't want to go on this way, Lord. I believe that Jesus is the Son of God, and that His blood cleanses me now from all unrighteousness. I accept Jesus Christ as my personal Savior. I choose to follow and serve You now for the rest of my life, in Jesus' name. Amen.

My Prayer for Healing:

Hallelujah and thank You, Father for everything that You have done for me. I have called upon Your name and am saved (Rom. 10:13). Thank You for forgiving me of my sins. I in turn forgive those who have sinned against me (Matt. 6:12). Father, You have loved and called me Your own (Isa. 43:1). You have given me access into the holy of holies (Heb. 10:19). Because You promised to meet all of my needs (Phil. 4:19), I humbly, but boldly make my request known to You (Matt. 18:4; Heb. 4:16). I stand in need of healing, Jehovah Raphael (Jer. 17:14). Since You have sent Your Word to heal me and deliver me of my destructions (Ps. 107:20), I accept the healing that Jesus' suffering has bought me. Father, Your Word cannot be broken. It accomplishes what You send it out to do (Isa. 55:11). Thank You for the wounds, bruises, chastisement, and stripes (Isa. 53:5) that have provided healing for my spirit, emotions, mental state, and body. I can believe that I receive healing (Mark 11:24) because I already have it (1 Pet. 2:24). Now, I call forth by faith the manifestation of my healing in the name of Jesus (Heb. 11:6). I grasp it and cling to it. I am healed; be glorified in me (1 Cor. 6:20). Thank You. Amen.

My Prayer for Finances:

Hallelujah and thank You Father for everything that You have done for me. I know that You want me to prosper and be in health, even as my soul prospers (3 John 1:2). I need a big financial breakthrough Lord. I know that You are my Shepherd and that I do not have to want (Ps. 23:1). I have sowed seed into Your kingdom, and I shall reap it (Gal. 6:7). Your holy Word says that when I give, it shall be given back to me: good measure, pressed down, shaken together, and running over will men give into my bosom (Luke 6:38). I praise You for sending forth Your Word to give me the treasures of darkness, and hidden riches in secret places (Isa. 45:3). You have called me by name, and I will receive them. I praise You because Your Word has come to rebuke the devourer. He cannot destroy the fruit of my ground (Mal. 3:11). Make me usable so that I may be a good steward over all of the blessings that You pour out upon me (Mal. 3: 10). I will not rob You (Mal. 3:9). I will give cheerfully to Your work (2 Cor. 9:7). I endeavor to put Your will above my own. I will seek Your kingdom and Your way of doing things, and then I know that Your Word will cause all of what I need to be added unto me (Matt. 6:33). I will work diligently with my hands and become financially stable (Prov. 10:4) as my soul prospers and becomes fat (3 John 1:2; Prov. 13:14). I will put to good use my talents so that I may be a profitable, good, and faithful servant who will yield a pleasing increase to Your kingdom. Father, please position me to become a ruler over many things and enter into Your joy (Matt. 25:21). I acknowledge and believe that You have given me benefits in the Spirit and in the natural (Ps. 103:2; Eph.1:3). Thank You. I receive Your great and precious promises by faith (2 Pet. 1:4).

My Prayer for Encouragement/Anxiety/Fear:

Hallelujah and thank You, dear God for everything that You have done for me. Whenever I am afraid, I will trust in You

(Ps. 56:3). When I am sad and weary with groaning, You will hear and receive my prayer (Ps. 6:6; 9). Father, some issues of life have frustrated and disappointed me. My countenance has fallen, but Your Word compels me to hope and give You the praise. I know that Your Spirit will lead me to the rock that is higher than I (Ps. 61:2). My mind is cluttered with the same events that have brought me to this burdensome place. My soul is broken, but You shall restore it, Lord (Ps. 23:3). My body is tired because of what I am going through, but You will increase my strength (Isa. 40:29). Father, at times I do not even feel like talking to anyone, but I know that I am to walk by faith, not by my feelings (2 Cor. 5:7). Right now I do not want to listen to anyone or anything, but once again, Your Word rescues me. You enable me to hear what the Spirit is saying to me (Rev. 2:7). I feel sick to my stomach, and the sadness is eating away at my appetite, but You have given me the ability to eat, drink, and be merry (Eccles. 8:15). I will feast on Your Word, and rivers of living water will flow from my belly (John 7:38). Father, I do not feel like going anywhere or doing anything, but Your Spirit inspires me to clap my hands and dance before You with rejoicing (Ps. 47:1; 149:3). Also, it is hard to sleep and I don't feel safe right now, but You have told me not to be afraid (Ps. 4:8). You said that when I lie down You would give me peace and sweet sleep (Ps. 3:24). I have been waiting to see the manifestation of my hope (Prov. 13:12), but I know that my desire shall come because Your Word will not return unto You void (Isa. 55:11). Your Word has accomplished in me to build myself up on my most holy faith (Jude 1:20). I will do as You say, Father. I will keep my mind on You, and be in perfect peace (Isa. 26:3). I will speak to myself in psalms, hymns, and spiritual songs while making melody to You in my heart (Eph. 5:19). I will wait on You and You will hear me (Ps. 40:1). Blessed be You, dear God for You have not turned away my prayer or Your mercy from me (Ps. 66:20). By faith I receive my deliverance in Jesus' name. Thank You. Amen.

My Prayer for Wisdom/Direction:

Dear Father, thank You. You said that if I ask You for wisdom, You would liberally give it to me (James 1:5). There are decisions that must be made, and I call upon You to aide me with instruction (Prov. 1:2). I apply my heart to understanding and cry out for knowledge (Prov. 2:3). Now, Lord, I will trust in You, and You will open Your mouth and direct my way (Prov. 3:5–6; 2:6). By my trusting You and receiving Your way, You will teach me wisdom and lead me in the right direction (Prov. 4:11–12). When I make decisions and choices, they will not be stressed. When I go forth, I will not be hindered. I will be wise, hear Your instructions (Prov. 8:33) and receive my answer. Thank You, Father for sending Your Word and answering my prayer.

My Prayer for Spiritual Warfare/Protection:

Hallelujah! Dear Father, I am so glad that no weapon formed against me shall prosper (Isa. 54:17). Hallelujah! I am the righteousness of God, by Christ Jesus (2 Cor. 5:21). Lord I know that I am protected in You. I hold Your Word as true. Therefore, I know that Your angel encamps round about me (Ps. 34:7). When my enemies come upon me to attack, they will stumble and fall (Ps. 27:2). You are my God and will not hand me over to their will. You deliver me from my strong enemy (Ps. 18:17), so I will not be afraid (Ps. 23:4). You are the glory and lifter of my head (Ps. 3:3). My heart will trust in You, so I will not be discouraged in times of warfare. With Your help, I will stand girded in my spiritual armor (Eph. 6:11), waiting on You, Lord with good courage (Ps. 27:14). I will clap my hands, praise You, then move at Your command (Ps. 47:1) because it is You who avengeth me and subdue my enemies under me (Ps. 18:47). The battle is Yours (1 Sam. 17:47). I am born of Your Spirit and have power (John 3:6; Acts 1:8). I use my power to tread upon the hierarchy of evil, and to bind the principalities and all wicked powers that persuade its children to rise up against me for Your namesake (Luke 10:19). Just as You overcame, so shall I (John 16:33). As You are, so am I in this world (1 John 4:17). I use my authority in You to release ____________________ (Example: Harassment on my job) from me (Matt. 18:18), and I bind this spirit and all of its coworkers with chains and fetters (Ps. 149:8) so tight that they cannot speak, see, move, or communicate in any way, but they can hear themselves being bound in the name of Jesus. I speak death to the seed that this wicked attack grew from (Prov. 18:21). Satan is a liar (John 8:44). God is glorious (Phil. 3:21). I am victorious (Rom. 8:37). I submit myself to You, Father and I resist these evil spirits. I will no longer be tormented by them. Now I bind myself to peace in this area of my life. I speak life restored to my ____________________ (Example: Emotions).

This victory was not won by might or by power, but by Your Spirit, and I thank You, Father (Zech. 4:6). Hallelujah! It is done in Jesus' name.

My Prayer When Fasting:

Dear Father, I submit the fast that You have chosen. Make me usable that I may accomplish Your will. I humble myself before You to chastise my soul with fasting, that I may loose the bands of wickedness from ____________________ (Person(s)/Situation who/that have been entangled in the enemy's snares.) I humble myself in fasting to undo the heavy burdens of the heavy-laden, to let the oppressed go free and to break every yoke. I submit to the fast that You have chosen that I may feed the poor, give hospitality to those You send my way, clothe the naked and not hide from family members when they need my help. Lord, I submit to getting myself together. I submit to refraining from putting burdens on people and talking about things that I do not know. I submit to being willing to help the afflicted. Please forgive me for violating the Sabbath, and doing what I wanted to, even though it was not necessary. Please help me to completely surrender to You during this time of consecration that I may go on strike from the ways of the flesh. Lord, I crucify my flesh from all of the things that it likes. I crucify my flesh from distrust and disrespect for Your Word, and also from ______________________ (Name Stronghold). For Your namesake, I crucify my flesh from everything that it is attracted to. I crucify my flesh from anything and everything that motivates me to indulge in carnality. I hide myself away to be alone with You and to learn of You. I fast for a purer more intimate walk with You. I surrender all that I am, to grow deeper in Your love that I may know the breadth, length, depth, and height of who You are (Eph. 3:17–18). I know that I can do this because You have given me all things that pertain to life and godliness (1 Pet. 1:3). Let my light rise in obscurity. Let my darkness be as the noonday. Guide me continually and satisfy my soul in drought. Make me like a watered garden, like a spring of water (Isa. 58:11). Father, I am delighted in You (Ps. 37:4). Thank You for this opportunity to submit to the fast that You have chosen, in Jesus' name. Amen.

My Prayer for Sons and Daughters:

Sweet Father, I dedicate my children to You. I thank You for Your great and precious promises that will help my son/daughter escape the corruption that is in this world through lust (1 Pet. 1:4). I boldly come before You (Heb. 4:16) and stand in agreement with what You have said and validated (Num. 23:19). My request is for You to save my children and break into pieces the oppressor in their lives (Ps. 72:4). Let me see Your great work in their lives and please allow them to see Your great glory (Ps. 90:16). Let them continue in Your work well after I am gone, and let their seed be established before You (Ps. 102:28). Increase me more and more, dear Father, and my children too (Ps. 115:114). My children are Your heritage and the fruit of my womb is Your reward. Make them like sharp arrows in the hand of a might archer that they may shoot straight into the bull's-eye of Your will. I will be happy because Your quiver will be filled with Young bold workers who are not ashamed of You. They will fearlessly silence the enemy in the gate with Your Word (Ps. 127:3-5). O Lord, thou art my God! I will exalt thee. I will praise Your name because You have done wonderful things and all of Your counseling is faithful and true. That is why I can trust whatever You say (Isa. 25:1). You have never lied to anyone (Num. 23:19). Father, I know that You will quickly deliver my son/daughter from the destroyer and send forth the wasters away from them (Isa. 49:17). You will take away my son/daughter who have been captured as prey from the terrible and mighty and deliver them. You will contend with those who contend with me and save my children (Isa. 49:25). You will cause those who oppress my son/daughter, to be struck with their own devices, and then they will know that You are my Lord, Savior, Redeemer, and the mighty God of Jacob (Isa. 49:26). I have taught my children about You, and my future descendants shall be taught about You as well and have great peace (Isa. 54:13). My sons shall come to me from the far corners of sin, and my daughters shall be nursed by my side from Your Word (Isa. 60:4). Though my son/daughter is away from You right now, they won't be for long because Your hand is not too short to reach out and save him/her. Your ear is not heavy or hard of hearing my prayer (Isa. 59:1). Thank You, Lord for everything. Amen.

Record a few prayers of your own below:

____

____

____

____

____

Pray without ceasing.

—1 THESSALONIANS 5:17

And all things, whatsoever ye shall ask in prayer, believing, ye shall receive.

—MATTHEW 21:22

And when ye stand praying, forgive, if ye have ought against any: that your Father also which is in heaven may forgive you your trespasses.

—MARK 11:25

PAGE *of* SINGLE-MINDEDNESS

PAGE *of* SINGLE-MINDEDNESS (CONT.)

1. And ye shall seek me and __________ me, when ye shall __________ for me with __________ your __________. (Jer. 29:13)
2. The __________ of the body is the eye. If therefore thine eye be __________, thy whole body shall be full of light. (Matt. 6:19)
3. __________ man can __________ two masters. For either he will __________ the one, and love the other; or else he will __________ __________ the one and __________ the other...(Matt. 6:24)
4. But __________ ye __________ the kingdom of God and his righteousness, and all these things shall be __________ unto you. (Matt. 6:33)
5. That your __________ should not stand in the wisdom of men, but in the __________ of God. (1 Cor. 2:5)
6. See that __________ render evil for evil unto any __________, but ever __________ that which is good, both among yourselves and to __________ men. (1 Thess. 5:15) __________ evermore. (1 Thess. 5:16) __________ without ceasing. (1 Thess. 5:17) In everything __________ thanks; for this is the will of God concerning you. (1 Thess. 5:18) __________ not the Spirit. (1 Thess. 5:19) Despise __________ prophesyings. (1 Thess. 5:20) __________ all things; __________ fast that which is __________. (1 Thess. 5:21) __________ from __________ appearance of evil. (1 Thess. 5:22) And the very God of Peace __________ you __________... (1 Thess. 5:23)
7. __________ yourselves therefore to God. __________ the devil, and he will flee from you. (James 4:7) __________ nigh (near) to God, and he will __________ nigh (near) to you. __________ your hands, ye sinners, and __________ your hearts, ye double minded. (James 4:8)
8. Whom having __________ seen, ye __________; in whom though now ye see him __________, yet __________, ye rejoice with __________ unspeakable and __________ of glory. (1 Peter 1:8) Receiving the __________ of your __________, even the salvation of your souls. (1 Peter 1:9)
9. Little children __________ yourselves from __________. (1 John 5:21)

PAGE *of* GROWTH

PAGE *of* SOULS

PAGE *of* REFRESHING

PAGE *of* SURRENDER

SHIELD *of* FAITH

For we walk by faith, not by sight.

—2 Corinthians 5:7

So then faith cometh by hearing, and hearing by the word of God.

—Romans 10:17

Now faith is the substance of things hoped for, the evidence of things not seen.

—Hebrews 11:1

Jesus said unto him, If thou canst believe, all things are possible to him that believeth.

—Mark 9:23

Looking unto Jesus the author and finisher of our faith; who for the joy that was set before him endured the cross, despising the shame, and is set down at the right hand of the throne of God.

—Hebrews 12:2

If ye have faith as a grain of mustard seed, ye shall say unto this mountain, Remove hence to yonder place; and it shall remove; and nothing shall be impossible unto you.

—Matthew 17:20

[22]And Jesus answering saith unto them, Have faith in God.
[23]For verily I say unto you, That whosoever shall say unto this mountain, Be thou removed, and be thou cast into the sea; and shall not doubt in his heart, but shall believe that those things which he saith shall come to pass; he shall have whatsoever he saith. [24]Therefore I say unto you, What things soever ye desire, when ye pray, believe that ye receive them, and ye shall have them.

—Mark 11:22–24

For therein is the righteousness of God revealed from faith to faith: as it is written, The just shall live by faith.

—Romans 1:17

But without faith it is impossible to please him: for he that cometh to God must believe that he is, and that he is a rewarder of them that diligently seek him.

—HEBREWS 11:6

For whatsoever is born of God overcometh the world: and this is the victory that overcometh the world, even our faith.

—1 JOHN 5:4

28And when he was come into the house, the blind men came to
him: and Jesus saith unto them, Believe ye that I am able to do
this? They said unto Him, Yea, Lord. 29Then touched he their
eyes, saying, According to your faith be it unto you.

—MATTHEW 9:28–29

14Is any sick among you? let him call for the elders of the church;
and let them pray over him, anointing him with oil in the name of
the Lord: 15And the prayer of faith shall save the sick.

—JAMES 5:14–15

For by grace are ye saved through faith; and that not of yourselves: it is the gift of God.

—EPHESIANS 2:8

Looking unto Jesus the author and finisher of our faith; who for the joy that was set before him endured the cross, despising the shame, and is set down at the right hand of the throne of God.

—HEBREWS 12:2

PAGE *of* ENCOURAGEMENT

God is our refuge and strength, a very present help in trouble.

—Psalm 46:1

The Lord is my shepherd; I shall not want.

—Psalm 23:1

The Lord is my light and my salvation; Whom shall I fear? the Lord is the strength of my life; Of whom shall I be afraid?

—Psalm 27:1

Yea, though I walk through the valley of the shadow of death, I will fear no evil: for thou art with me; thy rod and thy staff they comfort me.

—Psalm 23:4

I will instruct thee and teach thee in the way which thou shalt go: I will guide thee with mine eye.

—Psalm 32:8

Wait on the Lord: be of good courage, and he shall strengthen thine heart: wait, I say, on the Lord.

—Psalm 27:14

For he shall give his angels charge over thee, to keep thee in all thy ways.

—Psalm 91:11

Cast thy burden upon the Lord, and he shall sustain thee: he shall never suffer the righteous to be moved.

—Psalm 55:22

I waited patiently for the Lord; and he inclined unto me, and heard my cry.

—Psalm 40:1

The Lord is nigh unto them that are of a broken heart; and saveth such as be of a contrite spirit.

—Psalm 34:18

I sought the Lord, and he heard me, and delivered me from all my fears.

—Psalm 34:4

But the salvation of the righteous is of the Lord: He is their strength in the time of trouble.

—Psalm 37:39

The Lord hath heard my supplication; The Lord will receive my prayer.

—Psalm 6:9

I will not be afraid of ten thousands of people, that have set themselves against me round about.

—Psalm 3:6

My defense is of God, which saveth the upright in heart.

—Psalm 7:10

When mine enemies are turned back, they shall fall and perish at thy presence.

—Psalm 9:3

But know that the Lord hath set apart him that is godly for himself: The Lord will hear when I call unto him.

—Psalm 4:3

PAGE *of* PRAYER

PAGE *of* EDIFICATION

PAGE *of* COMFORT

He maketh me to lie down in green pastures: He leadeth me beside still waters. He restoreth my soul.

—Psalm 23:2–3

He hath delivered my soul in peace from the battle that was against me: for there were many with me.

—Psalm 55:18

Thou wilt keep him in perfect peace, whose mind is stayed on thee because he trusteth in thee. Trust ye in the Lord for ever: for in the Lord Jehovah is everlasting strength.

—Isaiah 26:3–4

Come unto me, all ye that labor and are heavy laden, and I will give you rest. Take my yoke upon you, and learn of me; for I am meek and lowly in heart: and ye shall find rest unto your souls. For my yoke is easy, and my burden is light.

—Matthew 11:28–30

Let not your heart be troubled: ye believe in God, believe also in me. In my Father's house are many mansions: if it were not so, I would have told you. I go to prepare a place for you. And if I go and prepare a place for you, I will come again, and receive you unto myself, that where I am, there ye may be also.

—John 14:1–3

Brethren, I count not myself to have apprehended: but this one thing I do, forgetting those things which are behind, and reaching forth unto those things which are before.

—Philippians 3:13

Casting all your care upon Him; for he careth for you.

—1 Peter 5:7

DREAMS, VISIONS, *and* SPIRITUAL INTERACTIONS *with* GOD

And it shall come to pass afterward, that I will pour out my spirit upon all flesh; and your sons and your daughters shall prophesy, your old men shall dream dreams, your young men shall see visions.

—Joel 2:28

Date:

___

___

___

Date:

___

___

___

Date:

___

___

___

Date:

___

___

___

Date:

Date:

Date:

(For additional journaling, you may download more resources from www.YhavinasHeart.com.)

ABOUT *the* AUTHOR

YHAVINA MCLENDON WAS an example of a true disciple of Jesus Christ. This is not merely a mother's opinion, but the testimony of those whose lives crossed paths with hers. I can testify to the fact that I saw favor on her in everything that she put her hands to. I remember her telling me that she wanted to seize the day, and she did. Yhavina had always been a good student and could draw very well, too. By the age of nineteen, God had given her many accomplishments. She was an active youth group member and church volunteer. She attended Oral Roberts University and was a National Dean's List recipient. Although Yhavina is no longer with us in body, the work that God did through her is still touching lives today.

She went to her eternal home in the spring of 2004. Throughout her illness she never complained, never became bitter and never kept silent. Yhavina continually witnessed to hospital staff, family, friends and even strangers about God's goodness until she could no longer speak with her mouth, she then used her eyes.

CONTACT *the* AUTHOR

YhavinasHeart@YhavinasHeart.com